MY LOYAL DOGS

By

OZOEMENA ISAAC

"There is no faith which has never yet been broken, except that of a truly faithful dog"

My loyal dogs by Ozoemena Isaac

. –Konrad Lorenz

To

All proud dog owners!

My loyal dogs by Ozoemena Isaac

My loyal dogs by Ozoemena Isaac

My loyal dogs by Ozoemena Isaac

Dog keeping

Keeping of dogs is something that has been there, a practice as old as history itself. Many peoples and cultures have kept dogs for various purposes.

Dogs have been human companions for ages. I doubt if one could define ancient hunting, without mention of dogs. Well trained dogs have been used for security, and many have proven their usefulness in times of war. In the twenty first century, dogs have been trained to do almost anything, sending and collection of mails from the mail post, dancing, babysitting, and much more. You can only tell from the angle you have experienced them. The fact still remains that dogs are the most kept pets since the history of pet keeping.

We have kept many dogs since I was an infant, there were some that we just kept, then sold, there were a few however, who were quite remarkable,. These ones proved in one way or another to be worthy of remembrance.

I shall try to tell the tales briefly, giving glory to those who deserved it, and I believe that at the end of this, you would give credit to the age long companions that are called dogs.

These are all memories, a true account of the times that have been.., of deeds that have made my my mind wonder the difference between us and other animals, for I have observed that they have their own reasoning, a sense of responsibility, the evidence of a mind, and manifestation of a soul, the power to love and be faithful..
~Ozoemena

Lion, my loyal friend

I don't know why, but animals seem to have this unquenchable affinity for children. Being the youngest in the house, our dog (lion) took to me. It would hardly let me out of its sight. As intimidating as the sight of her may seem, she still had a soft heart that accommodated even me. She had given birth many times, being randomly crossed with any of the stray male dogs walking the streets. She had one steady boyfriend, Okwu-bha-n'ego, a bull of a dog from the neighbouring clan. Lion hardly had time to go flirting around,all her time was given to staying with the family. She hated the prospect of being left alone at home.

My loyal dogs by Ozoemena Isaac

"The greatest fear dogs know is the fear that you will not come back
when you go out the door without them."
— **Stanley Coren**

My loyal dogs by Ozoemena Isaac

Life and stories of Ozoemena

Left at the   farm

I remember one certain incident. We took her to our farm at Iyi-kpokpo. She was so busy hunting around that she didn't know when we left. We came with boat and as we waited for her to no avail, we had to go home. That evening lion swam all the distance back, looking so beaten and downcast. I felt warm tears go down my cheeks. She immediately came to me. Seeing how I felt, her warm tongue reached for the back of my hand. I could feel the plea in her eyes , she needed company and she knew I was the only one who would understand her. She could not leave my side. I gave her part of my dinner that night. She slept outside my tent.

The next day we went visiting to Iyi-kpokpo our friends told us they heard the sound of a dog whelping near our farm. They said the dog stayed and cried out all it could but seemed to be lost and alone. I felt a soft part of my heart beat for my lion.

Lion in school

Lion had to be alone alone most of the week days as we left early for school each day, coming back late afternoon. One day when she could no longer bear our absence she tracked us to school. She entered our open classroom and everyone was scared. The teacher ran away from her table. I immediately recognized my lion and ran to her. I could see it in her eyes. I could feel her saying with her mind, "why did you have to leave me alone?" I looked into those sad eyes. I'm sorry, but I could not help leaving you at home. My sister and brother heard the commotion and came over from their classes. My sister was very angry she went out to get a stick to hit the dog to send her away. But lion would not go, she cowered in my arms.   I felt my anger rise at my sister. "leave my dog alone!" she stopped in her tracks. She was never used to me raising my voice at her. She didn't say anything again. Miss Comfort, their class teacher and close family friend, came over and could not control her laughter. She touched my arm. "Don't worry, I'll see your father, we need to get your dog her own uniform so she could be coming to classes with you!". Everyone laughed. Then gently,Miss Comfort convinced me to let the dog go. As the dog left, she had her ears slant and her head bowed. Why would they not allow her to stay with the people she loved and cared about? The sad glance she threw at my sister was enough to tell me she understood my anger. She turned and with one loyal wag of her tail, left the class.

That night my father could not hide his amusement. Yet I felt something when he looked at me. He saw something in my action, something in my action that he admired. The look in his eyes was very different from the mocking look I had gotten from most people earlier that day.

Lion no longer allowed me out of her sight, except for school and church. And funny enough, she forgot I was not a dog like her, and definitely not a puppy. She got into this habit of knocking me over each time we played.

Getting knocked over

One day at the farm, we decided to rest after working for hours. Lion was game. Immediately I shouted 'lion!' she answered with a bark. She was wagging all over. I knew what she was expecting next. I ran off and instantly she took off after me, reducing the distance between us with such speed that i did not think Bolt could afford. At just few months to my 9th birthday, I weighed next to nothing compared the heavily built lion. My brother and sister just sat and watched us. At a point I did not see her behind me again. I slowed my pace. But just then, "wham!" she sprang and knocked me clean off my feet. I rolled over the slope of heaped grasses, excited and overwhelmed. The next instant she was standing over me, like a prey ready for final sentence. She barked, almost a growl, and playfully sank her teeth into my belly. It didn't get deep, but I felt the sharp blades hit my skin and I pitied any animal or man that would make an enemy of my lion.

On another occasion lion was with my brother and sister down the stream. I had gone to see some friends. Immediately I reached the entrance to our compound my sister, so mischievous, yelled to the dog "get him!" I screamed and ran. Lion barked and leaped into the air. The stream was almost fifty yards away from the entrance, but in less than a minute lion had covered the distance. My slippers flew into the air, I was discharging every encumbrance that would predispose me to lion's sharp teeth. I ran into the house and speedily ran into my tent. But just as I was about crawling in, I felt lion's sharp teeth on my legs. She held very firmly, yet gentle enough not to cut my skin. She dragged me out from the tent and gave a very loud growl,like ,"gotcha!" I was brought back from my shock by her wet warm tongue on my face. In her mind she must be saying ,"this one is still a kid, my kid boy when will you grow up?"

Another thing lion did very perfectly was swimming. Born and bred in the camp, She could swim more than the fish themselves. On most hot afternoons, when only the cool waters of the stream seemed to hold the solutions, we would jump into the cold waters. Feeling left out, poor lion would jump in too. For a good deal of time, I watched the dog swim, all four legs moving through the water, with just the head above water, lion was an excellent swimmer, and she enjoyed swimming with us, because even in the water, she still bit and lashed out playfully with her teeth.

Who is stealing the eggs?

But Lion had a habit that my father had to flog out of her..

My father had many birds, domestic birds. They laid eggs every now and then. But something happened, some of the eggs started to disappear. My father got furious. After interrogating each of us, he laid a trap and caught lion eating the eggs. The next day he caught lion and chained her to the biggest tree in our compound. There was no type of stick he did not hit her with that day. At a point I joined lion to cry, but an angry look and a growl from my father got me running for cover. I could never forget the tears my dog shed that day. But the thing is, after that day, eggs disappeared no more. My father had decided not to spare the rod and spoil the dog.

Pregnant lion

After many visits from her boyfriend, lion finally took in. As her pregnancy advanced she became restless and easily irritated. Her swollen red vulva seemed to want to bulge out of her body. I pitied her so much because I understood from the mist in her eyes each time she glanced at me, that she wasn't having it easy. After the stressful period that seemed like it would never end, my father woke us up one morning to say that lion had finally put to bed around midnight. The next day we cooked her a special meal to welcome her back from the mountain of pregnancy and labor. The puppies, about seven of them, looked so very tender, so innocent and beautiful. We immediately shared the puppies among us. Lion never hid her pleasure seeing the care we showered on her children. The fine face of a He-goat does not prevent him from being taken to the market when needs start knocking at the door of the owner. About a month after their birth, my father began to sell them out.   He eventually sold them all, leaving lion childless once again. But the poor dog was not one to complain. She accepted her fate.

"Look not with hate upon those that I love.."

After the farming season was over, we spent more time visiting our friends and hunting games. One day one of my close friends Charles came to see me at home. We talked and played for long. Then I challenged him to a wrestling match. He accepted. As we both began the struggle, it appeared we were going to have a draw, as tactics conjured by one was sharply countered by the other. When lion saw us struggling, and the way Charles was grabbing me, she felt I was in danger and in an instant she was on her feet. The hair rose in a ridge on her back and her teeth flashed in an angry snarl. Then she barked! I saw drops of emergency piss reaching down from Charles' shorts. 'hold your wolf!"

Lion had already crouched on rippling muscles, ready to pounce when we hastily disengaged and I ran to her. I held and patted her. "don't worry he won't hurt me" I whispered softly into her ears as my fingers smoothed the risen hair on her back. She wagged her tail but still kept a watchful eye on Charles. Charles could not contain his fear anymore, he left on shaky legs for his own safety.

When a dog fights victoriously..

One Saturday evening I had gone to see a friend and on my way back home, I saw a dog that looked exactly like lion. I began to call her name and whistle. To my chagrin the dog did not come to me as my lion would have. It just stood there and looked at me, seeming to enjoy my confusion. Then it began to get approach me, with a look that was neither familiar nor friendly. The next moment I saw lion jump in, with her teeth bare, and all the hair on her body standing at attention. I shifted back as lion moved in to face the other dog. In that brief moment I saw the difference, lion had a lighter brown. I could see her fury. How dare this intruder try to scare my boy! She charged. Both dogs bit and snarled at each other. Lion had the advantage of speed. The other dog started squealing, lion had probably bitten it at a sensitive spot. Then it fell. Lion showed no mercy. But when I thought she was going to kill the intruder, she decided to let go. The intruder ran away with a limp and the tails between its legs. "my lion!" I ran to lion and gave her a passionate pat on the head.

Lion, was a true lioness when it came to fighting. Of over twenty five battles she had engaged in my presence, she never lost any. Her back had never reached the ground in any fight before.

My loyal dogs by Ozoemena Isaac

"

Life and stories of Ozoemena

Dogs die. But dogs live, too. Right up until they die, they live. They live brave, beautiful lives. They protect their families. And love us. And make our lives a little brighter. And they don't waste time being afraid of tomorrow."
— Dan Gemeinhart, The Honest Truth

They understand..

One day my sister gave me a very heartless flogging, one that left me with many emotional and physical wounds that the scares took months to disappear. I could not exactly remember what my offence was. I cried so bitterly and ran to the stream where I for an undisturbed couple of hours, I had my peace of mind. Not long after I got to the stream, crouched low on the sharp sand at the edge of the stream, I felt a warm tongue at the back of my neck. I turned sharply, to see lion. The look in her eyes were one of pity, and a deep compassion that could not be spoken. Her came right in front of me and with her weight settled on my stretched out legs. She didn't take her eyes away from mine. It understood and felt the gravity of my sadness. Beneath the strength and roughness of the lioness in her, lay a deep softness that touched a cord in embittered heart. I understood. If it had been a stranger that had raised a finger on me, she'd have torn the person to pieces. But my sister was family, lion had limits to her brutal defensiveness. At the thought of this I tried to brighten up. Lion , as if she was reading my mind, chose that time to growl, one of her special playful growls. I got up and ran off in the direction of the forest. In an instant she was on her feet. As I thought I was gaining speed over her, she slacked her speed and crouched. I did not notice she had stopped. I was so deafened by the waves that I didn't hear her coming. But the next moment   she came crashing down on me. We both came crashing to the ground. "you brute! Won't you ever quit knocking me over??" , I yelled. She barked playfully and started biting playfully at my small hand. And I was laughing and smiling again!

My loyal dogs by Ozoemena Isaac

"Thorns may hurt you, men desert you, sunlight turn to fog;
but you're never friendless ever, if you have a dog."
— **Douglas Malloch**

Lion the second (Black lion)

Before we became friends..

In Ogidi, mama kept only males. She said she had not the time to control a full house of dogs and their puppies. Most of the males she had castrated, to reduce the chances of them jumping out in search of females. The first dog I met in mama's house was a huge black dog, with hair that covered his eyes and a body weight that gave a great thud to his steps. The mere sight of him alone was threatening. The first day I came to Ogidi I was scared to my marrows. They usually got him locked inside his cage during the daytime and released at night. That made evenings periods of horror to me the first few weeks that I came to Ogidi to stay with mama. Most times I would hold back urine for hours until daybreak when the huge black dog would be locked in. The way it barked made the chills run down my spine. Despite having had a dog before, this one looked so very different from all other dogs I had seen so far. In my child's eye it looked heartless.

When mama noticed how much I dreaded this dog, she began to give me the dog's food to personally give to him. At first I did this from a distance. When mama saw this, she instructed my elder brother staying with us then to acquaint me with the dog. How he chose to do it really scared the shit out of me. In the evening, with me hiding behind him, he would release the dog and then ask me to pat the dog on the head. Fear never allowed me to look the dog in the eye not to talk of touching it. And the poor animal seemed excited by the presence of a child in the house. It would bark and rush for me, these had me wetting my pants. My brother tried to assure me the dog meant no harm. But I didn't think so, not with a dog that roared like a real lion.

Friends

After about three days of repeating the same process, I made up my mind to reach out and touch the dog. The dog seemed so excited that I touched it. Then it rose on its hind legs, almost my height at the time and gave my face a lick. From that moment we became friends. the black lion grew so very fond of me. On most cold days he would come and climb on to my laps and curl up. He made a great companion. I shared my food with him most days, and he got accustomed to having a taste of whatever I ate, even when he would not touch his own food.

Lion was a good hunter, that hardly any week passes that we would not see a grasscutter at our door. Lion was not a vindictive dog. Sometimes we found the head or tail missing, but that was all he would take for his troubles. Lion never stole. He had a strict definition of morality and he stuck to it. Never for once did any thing disappear under Lion's watch, be it meat or fish or whatever would have made other dogs stumble.

Something happened however, that embedded the image of the huge black dog on my soul.

The great loss..

One certain season, the fleas and ants infestation got too much for him. I bought an insecticide that I was supposed to put in his bath water. Unfortunately there were no specifications about quantity. So out of eagerness to get my dog freed from the ticks and other ants that made his life miserable, I poured almost half into the water I was going to bath him with. I had planned to use the other half the following day. I hated to see my dog suffer. Sometimes the scratching got him sores and flies.

After bathing him, I let him go dry himself as usual, but after about five minutes my dog staggered back. I rushed to him. His eyes showed pain and his breath unsteady. I watched him fall. It was then I realized that the handshake had gone beyond the wrist. The reality hit me. the concentration was probably too much, and the poor dog had licked his body in an attempt to dry up I cried out. Mama suggested oil. I rushed and started feeding him oil. That didn't help. It dawned on me that my dog was gradually leaving me. He could hardly move anything but his eyes. With my dying dog in my arms, I wept aloud. Then something happened, I saw real tears drop from my dog's eyes. I watched it roll down and slowly, those eyes lifted feebly for one last look at me, then closed forever. I screamed and threw myself to the ground. I could not control my grief. It was bad enough that the dog died, but those tears it shed and that last look, made my heart bleed. It took mama a lot of persuasion to get me off the ground, and to let go of the dog. As I dug the big whole that would be his grave that evening, I could not hold back tears. I mourned him as I would mourn a true friend. His loyalty was total, and his love was untainted, and most painfully, it was my fault, my error that cut his sweet life short.

White 'Thunder'

After him we had many other dogs, worth mentioning is the fierce white 'thunder' that tore iron with his teeth, great hunter he was , and had incorrigible sense of independence. He had not much hair, but I can bet you that if you used his skin for drum, it would last a century! He knew no such thing as pain. He went where he wanted, if you tried to restrict him he'd break or eat down the door. Dogs I realize, do not like being kept away from the people they cared for. I was told that about two of the dogs mama had before I came, were killed by lightening as they broke down their iron door and tried to get out on a rainy evening. They had tried to get out, and as they came across the huge palm tree that gave shade to their house, lightening struck and cut them and the palm tree down. Maybe it was the similarity of this white dog to the ones that thunder killed that influenced the decision to name him 'thunder'. His independence got him jumping our 8 feet fence to go mate with females. On one of these escapades of his, he got into a trap, and never survived it.

Jimmy the faithful

In 2012, long after the death of 'thunder' mama decided it was time to get another dog. She had a friend who had dogs that bred hybrid puppies every season. This time I went myself. As I entered the compound, the puppies raised alarm and then one of them ran to me. I could not touch it then because the mother was nearby, it might misconstrue my show of affection for something else. But I marked the particular puppy that came to me. That's mine!

As I paid mama's friend, I searched out the puppy. The girl that lived with the woman helped me put the dog in my bagco a nd we commenced the journey home. I had to trek. So I brought out the dog and carried it in my arms like a baby. He had this look of mixed feelings in his eyes. I understood. He was going to miss his mother, he had tears in his innocent puppy eyes. I felt for it. I remembered the first time someone took me away from my mom.

"heyyyyv :-)" I smiled at the dog. " don't worry, I understand your feelings. I've been through this myself. I promise I would be your mom, your brother, and your family, from this moment on. I guarantee you my love and affection, and tolerance, and I will protect you, always, as much as I have the power to.." my eyes grew misty as I said the last sentence. Can I protect the dog from his own fears, seen and unseen? I do not know for sure, but to the best of my ability, I would give him a better tomorrow. The dog, as if it read my thoughts, whined and feebly wagged his tail. Dogs are indeed very lovely at their tender age.

With time Jimmy grew. He grew in an extra ordinary way. I had given him so much care, he considered himself a human. He even learned to pose for pictures. He grew into something huge, with a threatening presence.

We got so attached, that even after I got admission into the university, and stayed some months away, he never forgot me. He would even sense my presence from miles away any weekend I would travel home. Then he would come wait at the gate and his eyes flashing unspeakable happiness at the sight of me. Entering the university had separated us physically, but we were much in touch emotionally. His sleeping position changed each time I went home. He would curl up at my door, and some nights slip in without my knowing. I would only wake up to the sounds of him shaking himself, and a triumphant glaze in his eyes.

Then he learned a new thing, he noticed that most of the times I would come home, I would carry bag, and when I would go back to school I would be carrying bag too. So he began to watch me, any day he saw me carry my backpack and go towards the gate, he would rush and grab my leg, then gently drag me back inside. I could feel the plea in his eyes. 'don't go..' The first time he did this I almost wept. I had to go back inside and pet him until his attention got off the backpack, then I slipped away. With time this became I challenge I had to face each time I would travel back to school. Aside from his closeness, Jimmy was disciplined and just as one could see from his appearance, a mighty dog. He was meek and gentle, yet strong and brutal when the purpose suited him.

After mama's demise Jimmy was sold. This happened while I was away at school. I came back and found that Jimmy was gone. In my closet I shed some tears for my loyal friend, for the good times we had together, for the jolly fellow he was , and the regret that I wasn't able to save him. This dog so much reminded me of my black lion. There was not much I could do, but keep moving on. I knew he would want me to move on and be happy, that's Jimmy's way.

THE IANIS BROTHERS AND THE CHAINS

In mid 2017 we bought two puppies. I was away at the university at the time. I came back to meet the puppies. Due to my kind of person, it was believed that I could handle any animal, added to the fact that I studied zoology, ecology and bio-conservation option.

At home they found it hard to get the little puppies bathed. The dogs trusted no one to come too close , not to talk of coming with sponge and water.   During one of our phone discussions dad had mentioned the puppies and tactically pushed it indirectly to me , the responsibility of getting the dogs to agree to get bathed.

So I got home on one fine weekend and like magic the dogs took a liking to me. I got fascinated too. They were the perfect police dogs. Threateningly sharp teeth that flashed in splits of a second; hair that got theirs eyes half covered. They had enough looks to scare the lilies out of anyone who does not know their onions in "dog science" The next day I had them bathed.

Now came the main trouble.. time to get the chains on!

I was still away at the university, awaiting the christmas break when daddy called me one Friday afternoon to complain that the dogs had gone completely wild. One of them had scratched him badly in a playful brawl. They never seemed to have understood that we humans don't have thick skin like them. Dad said the Ianis brothers had gotten so uncontrollable that they never allowed themselves to be coerced into their cages anymore, with or without bait, tricks and whims, all to naught. They now even bark at even daddy himself. For a second a feeling of pride surged through my veins. *my puppies have grown...*

As I got home that Christmas I could not recognize them anymore. Three months away had wiped whatever recognition and comradeship I had built with them. They barked wildly at me. I knew that if I must enjoy my holiday I had to establish an understanding between us. So the next day I got set. They vehemently rebuffed all attempts to get close or even touch them. They would not even accept gifts of meat and bones directly from me. They simply trusted no one. I could feel the ruggedness of their corrugated willpower. At a point I approached,   and they barked and growled so violently I thought they were going to attack. Then suddenly i had an idea. Dogs don't have human language, but they understand gestures! So I bent one knee and crouched beside the newly bought heap of sharp sand close in the open frontage. As I crouched and stretched my two hands towards them they stopped barking. Call it surrender or whatever you like, I had just showed them I was harmless and they understood. The next moment they came close and after rounds of sniffing my hand and face, began to pull at my hand playfully. And that was it. We played like mad. I was with both hands and legs on the ground, like them. So as they approached I would dodge the rush and try squeezing their hair. they were splashing sand and running round and round and trying to pull at my cloths or any part of my body without getting caught or squeezed by my swift outstretched hands.

Moments later I was at the sink trying to rinse out as much sand as I could from my eyes. But I achieved my aim. *We are comrades again!.*

The next day I set out on actualizing my plan of getting the dogs chained. I got to our playing arena, and once again I showed my loyalty, crouching on all fours and stretching my hands out before me. As they reciprocated doing the the same, I got the chains out of the bag. They still did not suspect anything. I tied my waist with the chain and showed them the chain on my waist. We continued to play. They were even pulling the chain and almost dragging me. It excited them that I played with them as one of their own, I knew I had their trust, and I was going to play on it. As their excitement peaked, I gently slid the chains from my waist, then stealthily on one and then on the other. i tried to continue the play, but then they had already realized what happened.. they had been tricked. Betrayed!.

Their countenance immediately changed. They backed away from me, and wore very long faces. They would not even ,move. To my chagrin, they began to hide. Their freedom had been taken away, and they believed that spelled imminent danger.

What broke my heart however, was what happened next. My favorite of the two, who would normally have stuck with me, even if it was raining buffalo, ran away from me. Then he ran into an abandoned car tire and began to whelp. He cried at the top of of his voice. It was a cry of pain, of deep disappointment. I had betrayed his trust, their trust. I got food and bones and tried to pacify them but they ran farther away from me. My favorite cried all the more, with a very sad, melancholic voice. It was quite different from the sound of pain a dog would make when you flog it. This was deeper, I had hurt him to his depth, like Brutus I had delivered the final stroke that broke his heart. I tried all I could but no way. They had me blocked out of their heart. Even when I tried to get close and try to touch them, they would be shaking terribly as if they feared I was going to slit their throats. One always starts urinating impulsively on seeing me come close. I knew I had become a symbol of danger and evil to the dogs. We were back to square one.

I travelled back to school with the guilt nagging at me. I had betrayed my friends. But I tried to take solace that dad was the one wnho asked me to do it and I believed I did it for their good.

Friends ever after

The next time I travelled home, I had this resolve to vindicate myself. I must regain the trust of my loyal friends, I must prove to them that I did not betray them on purpose.

Immediately I got home I reached to them. I saw that dad had removed the chains. I guess that was why they did not fully ignore me. Like babies they forgave, but I had doubts that they would forget so easily. So I got down to business. Throughout that evening I played with them. I repeated that the next two days. And slowly their confidence returned. They decided probably to give me another chance, and I took it with both hands, I was never going allow anybody bring tears to my friends' eyes again! They saw this through out that season and the season that followed. Each time I travelled , they felt happy and they would never leave my door. Most times they would curl up at my door for the night. The bond that existed between us returned, this time even much stronger.

My loyal dogs by Ozoemena Isaac

Did you enjoy this story? Feel free to tell me how you feel at
ozoemenaisaac5@gmail.com

I would gladly welcome your suggestions and constructive criticism.

Other stories by Ozoemena

The Mystical Crush , available on Amazon.

Paperback available from here Mystical Crush paper back

Life and stories of Ozoemena

You can also follow me on Amazon for to get first hand notifications of my latest releases see Ozoemena Isaac Amazon Author page